Sir Lived Alot

And the Quest for the Golden Happy Face

Written and illustrated by
Zoe Carter

Copyright 2016

The Bible is a great big library. Sixty-six
books in all. Some are big and some are small.

Books about the past, books about the future,
letters, poems, stories that are true. And all the
books are from God to you.

Take a look at this book. It's called Ecclesiastes.

'That is such a sad poem', said Little Owl.

'Life can be very sad', said Wise Owl.

'Ecclesiastes was written by King Solomon. He had everything but he didn't feel happy.'

'I don't understand', said Little Owl.

'Sometimes the best way to understand a difficult idea is to tell a good story...'

Once upon a time there was a boy who dreamed of becoming a knight.

So when he grew up, that is exactly what he did.

Every knight needs a quest, so on a quest he went:
to find the Golden Happy Face.

Round and round the world he went. Where could that Golden Happy Face be?

He was young and handsome, with his whole life
in front of him.

Everything he wanted he ate it; he bought it.

He danced all night and slept all day.

And his life became filled with happy bubbles.

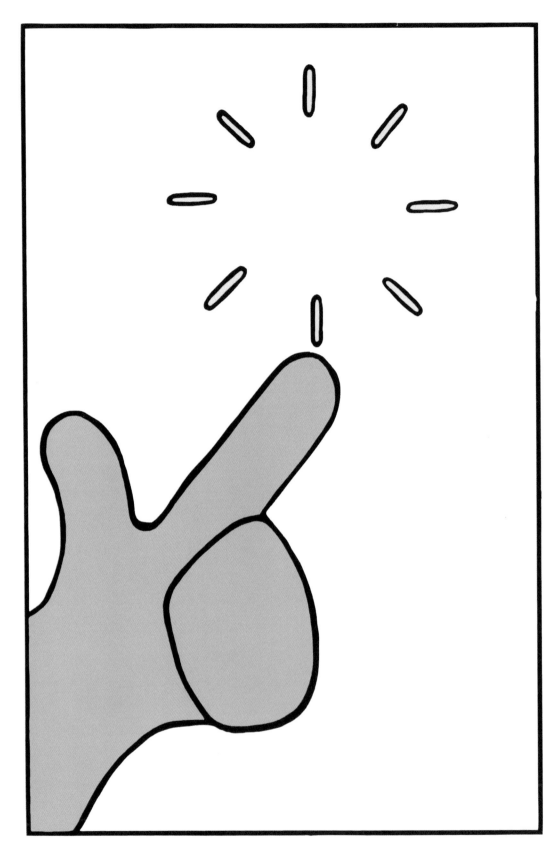

The bubbles were real. The bubbles were happy. But the bubbles popped. No matter how hard he tried, he couldn't hold a bubble close to him.

He grew a little older and a little wiser. He ate well and saved his pennies.

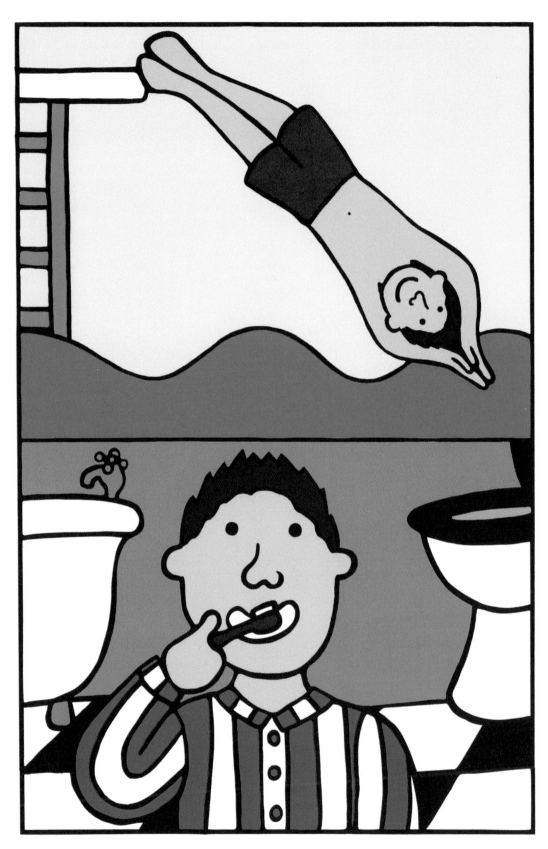

He exercised and brushed his teeth.

Still, he just found happy bubbles.
No Golden Happy Face.

He met a beautiful woman.

And he made her his wife.

He had a family of his very own.

He built a castle.

He slew a dragon.

His fame grew throughout the land. Everbody loved him.

Up and up the ladder of success he climbed. What was he going to find at the top? He found...

Nothing. Absolutely nothing at all.

He sunk to the ground in despair.

'Meaningless, meaningless!', he cried. 'Everything is meaningless, like chasing after the wind.'

He stopped believing in the Golden Happy Face.
'It's a fairy tale, like Cinderella and Snow White.
There is nothing but happy bubbles',
he said to himself.

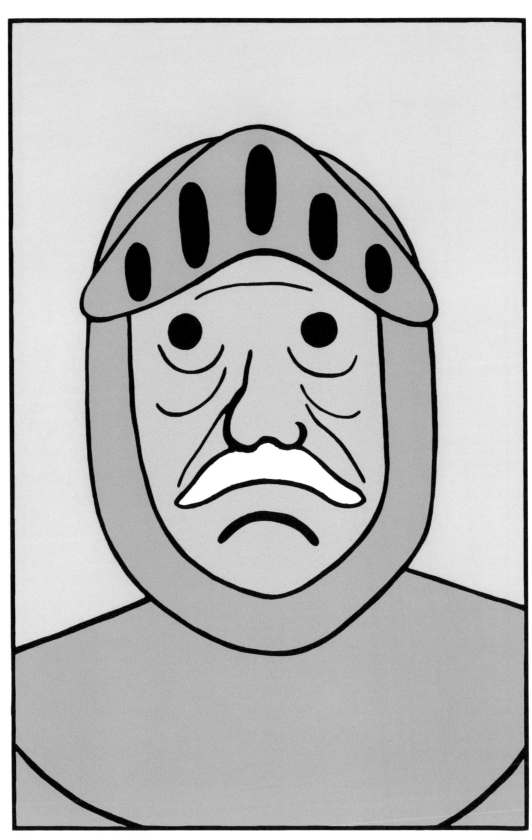

He called himself 'Sir Lived Alot' because he
had seen it all. He had become old.

And so had his wife.

But this is not the end of the story. One day he got an invitation to tea with the King.

He told the King all about his lifelong quest for the Golden Happy Face, and how he realised there was no such thing.

The King's eyes shone with delight as he passed him a book. 'I have written this for you. See what's inside'.

Sir Lived Alot opened the book, and inside he found the Golden Happy Face.

He could not believe his eyes. 'It's real',
he said. 'I knew it.'

'Thankyou. Thankyou ever so much.'

'And now we must be on our way. Goodbye.'
'Wait', said the King, 'Come back!'

Sir Lived Alot opened the book and saw that the further away he got from the King, the more the Golden Happy Face began to fade.

'You see, the golden happy face isn't a thing you take home. The golden happy face comes when you come close to me.'

'So leave your old life behind and come and live with me.
For I have prepared a place for you to live with me forever.'

Zoe Carter lives in Edinburgh, the capital of Scotland. She loves to make puppets, drink tea with her friends, and dress up in fancy dress costumes. Her favourite animal is an octopus.

www.zoecraftbook.com

Check out Zoe's Bible craft activity website www.zoecraftbook.com
More than 100 craft activities with full step by step photographic
instructions and templates. Fun, high quality and easy. Suitable for boys
and girls. Ideal for Sunday school, church, holiday clubs, homeschooling,
family time, VBS, camps, away days and many more.

Printed in Great Britain
by Amazon